OTL

Character Counts!

Michael Josephson

WITHDRAWN

The Best Is Yet to Come

More Thoughts on Living a Better Life and Being a Better Person

Michael Josephson

Joseph and Edna Josephson Institute of Ethics
Marina del Rey, California
2002

Published by the Josephson Institute of Ethics

Copyright ©2002 by Michael Josephson

All rights reserved under International and Pan-American Copyright Conventions. Published in the United States by the Josephson Institute.

www.charactercounts.org / www.josephsoninstitute.org

CHARACTER COUNTS! is a service mark of the **CHARACTER COUNTS!** Coalition, a project of the Josephson Institute.

ISBN 1-888689-14-5

Publisher's Cataloging-in-Publication
(Provided by Quality Books, Inc.)

Josephson, Michael S., 1942-
    The best is yet to come : more thoughts on being a
better person and living a better life / Michael
Josephson. -- 1st ed.
    p. cm.
    ISBN 1-888689-14-5

    1. Character.   I. Title.

BJ1521.J67 2002   170
                               QBI02-701496

Manufactured in the United States of America
First Edition

Contents

Sources and Attribution

My primary goal as a teacher is to inform, stimulate, inspire and touch readers and listeners. To do this I use a wide array of parables, stories, anecdotes, metaphors and poems. Some of them (including all those written in the first person and those taken from news stories or other sources I consider reliable) are true to the best of my knowledge. Others are based on stories I've heard or read elsewhere. With these stories, I cannot tell whether they are true accounts or parables created to teach a particular lesson. In a few cases I have used such stories intact, but in most I rewrite extensively, hoping to make a particular point more clearly or emphatically. Finally, many of the stories and poems were written by me, as my daughter Carissa says, "out of my head."

Though I provide the source when I know it, I have sometimes been unable to identify a poem's author or a story's origin. With so many stories and versions of stories circulating on the Internet and in e-mails, and with so many books of stories on the market today, it can be very difficult to identify sources.

If you know the original source of any unattributed materials, please forgive my ignorance and send me the information (by e-mail to michaeljosephson@jiethics.org). We'll correct future editions.

Acknowledgments

I want to again acknowledge and thank all the people of the Josephson Institute team who have played vital roles in the production of the radio commentaries and their translation into this book. Very special thanks to Lauren Fair, my administrative assistant who expands my capacity tenfold; to Tom DeCair, who has organized and administered the commentaries and our relationships with the radio stations carrying them; to Terry Harrison, who helped select, edit and organize the commentaries in this volume; to Wes Hanson, who designed the cover and page layout, and has overseen the entire editing and publishing effort; to John Auld, a longtime friend and adviser whose company, Pace Publications in Anaheim, California, printed this book; to Steve Nish, who has kept the commentaries accessible in text and audio form on our web page (www.charactercounts.org); to Todd Katzberg, who organizes and sends out our weekly e-mail of the commentaries; to Dan McNeill, who with Steve and Todd provided crucial editing services; to Cory Izquierdo, who responds to inquiries about the commentaries; and to Marjorie Tibar and Ed Uyehara, who manage the complex data collection and distribution of our growing list of subscribers.

Introduction

This volume of 64 essays is the sequel to my first book, *You Don't Have to Be Sick to Get Better!*. In the introduction to that volume I gave a good deal of personal history, stressing that my primary motivation and inspiration to explore the many facets of ethics and character come from my relationships, particularly with my parents, my children and my wife.

This fact is worth restating, because my formal education as a lawyer and my later lives as a business entrepreneur and law professor do not give me exceptional credentials to pontificate about right and wrong. Nor do I claim to be of extraordinary character myself. Rather, I am an ordinary man with the luxury of time to think and talk about living a good life in its fullest sense, the same issues I personally struggle with in my own quest to become a better person.

Michael Josephson

These essays are based on my daily commentaries, now carried by more than a dozen stations, including my home station, KNX-1070 AM in Los Angeles. I selected and occasionally rewrote them to present an experience that I hope you will find pleasurable, and at least occasionally enlightening, uplifting and touching.

I placed heavy emphasis in this volume on family and business relationships, as well as strategies for thinking about and living a good life, with the special hope that new graduates and parents will find it of particular value.

Reflecting on the unexpected success of my radio commentaries and the last book, I've come to realize I owe a debt of gratitude to Jack Canfield and Victor Hansen, the creators of the *Chicken Soup for the Soul* series. When this series became hugely successful, my first reaction was a combination of professional superiority (I thought some of the stories were corny) and just plain envy.

Yet, on more honest reflection, I realize how important it is that these men, drawing from their experiences as motivational speakers, understood the value of reintroducing our culture to simple personal stories as a means of teaching and touching not just the mind, but the heart. They generated a whole new genre of anecdotes and narratives laden with moral lessons. They gave teachers like me permission to go beyond reason and logic and tap into the full emotionality of human experience in a way that reminds us of our softer side, even to the point of drawing tears.

One of my favorite *Chicken Soup* stories is about a young boy who was asked to give blood by his mother to save his little sister's life. He was scared, but very brave. After a while, as the blood was being drained from his veins, he shocked the nurse when he solemnly asked her, "How much longer before I die?" Apparently, when he consented to the transfusion, he thought he had to give her all his blood — and yet he was willing to do that for his sister.

I cried when I first read the story, and the tears well up again as I retell it now. I don't really know whether it actually happened exactly this way. And it probably doesn't matter. These stories like many of mine are essentially parables, teaching devices that help us understand, encourage us to do better, and remind us of things we know but don't think about often enough.

William Arthur Ward said: "The mediocre teacher tells. The good teacher explains. The superior teacher demonstrates. The great teacher inspires." I aspire to inspire. I try to do that with touching stories and with observations and insights that challenge people to think more deeply about their lives.

I think these sorts of stories, and even my moralistic, sometimes preachy sermonettes on the power of principle and the value of virtue, are needed antidotes to the toxic cynicism that pervades popular culture.

We are battered regularly by so many reminders of the selfish, corrupt and cruel side of human nature that many of us begin to measure humanity by its weaknesses rather than its strengths. We need to be reminded that the love, self-sacrifice, integrity and courage of ordinary people confirm the extraordinary human capacity for nobility and prove that cynicism is a deplorable lie.

I believe that the source of our sentimental reaction is a passion for goodness that lives deep within all of us. Perhaps we cry at these warm stories, not simply because we feel joy in acts of love and honor, but because we are also a bit sad about not being as good as we could be. Fortunately, every day brings new opportunities to heed the voice of our souls and to find purpose and meaning in acts of virtue.

The title of the book, *The Best Is Yet to Come*, is intentionally upbeat. It is meant to stress the bright side of life, not based on mindless optimism, but on the practical reality that there are so many wonderful things ahead of us if we choose to focus on our families and our character. The title also goes with the cover photo of a butterfly just emerging from its cocoon, ready in its new form to experience the freedom of flight. That photo is symbolic of one of my favorite stories in the book about the mother who tries to help a butterfly, and ends up preventing it from growing strong wings.

Thank you for joining me on this continuing journey. And, in the end, I hope you will believe even more strongly that character counts.

— *Michael Josephson*
Los Angeles, California
March 2002

The Journey of Life: The Best Is Yet to Come

To finish the moment, to find the journey's end in every step of the road, to live the greatest number of good hours, is wisdom.

Ralph Waldo Emerson

Keep Your Fork: The Best Is Yet to Come

As the American journalist Sydney Harris put it, "A cynic is not merely one who reads bitter lessons from the past; he is one who is prematurely disappointed in the future." Thus, told that there will be a light at the end of the tunnel, the pessimist agrees, but assumes it will be coming from an onrushing train. I run into plenty of pessimists and they are rarely happy.

I think Samuel Johnson had it right when he observed that hope is itself a species of happiness. So if we want to be happy it only makes sense to discipline ourselves to choose our attitudes, to think positively and to be hopeful.

There's a story about a woman I've named Tilly who lived into her nineties as a positive thinker. When she died her family found explicit instructions for her funeral. She was to be dressed in her finest dinner clothing with a fork in her right hand. When anyone asked about the fork, which most did, the pastor was instructed to hand them an envelope containing the following note from Tilly:

"I'm glad you asked about the fork. I've attended hundreds of dinners. I noted that just when the dishes and flatware for the main course were being cleared, someone would always say, 'Keep your fork.' I loved that part because I knew that I needed my fork because dessert, the best part of dinner, was coming. So the fork in my hand is to remind you what I know and want you to believe: the best is yet to come."

Graduation: The Door to More and Better

A common observation made to young graduates is that they will look back on their school days as the best of their lives. And, to be sure, many wonderful memories will always connect them to this exciting, dynamic and often traumatic period of growth.

But to tell young people, on the threshold of adulthood, that the best years are behind them is an unkind lie that pollutes the sentiments associated with leaving friends and familiar surroundings with fear and apprehension about the future. The truth is much more encouraging: the best is yet to come. Graduation is the door to a life of more and better.

I urge graduates to think fondly of school memories, but also to rush enthusiastically into the future. Graduation marks the end of one chapter, but it's also a beginning, filled with unpredictable pleasures.

First, in many ways, the world outside school is kinder and fairer. Free from the pecking order of the school's social system, you are more likely to be judged for who you are and what you can do, rather than who you hang out with, what clubs you're in or how you dress. Natural insecurities will gradually surrender to self-confidence, and you will like yourself more when you learn that you don't have to be phony, rich, beautiful or even popular to live a good life.

You will keep old friends as long as you have things in common, but you are sure to make new ones as well. Yes, you will face additional challenges and responsibilities, but as a result, you will continually gain far greater control over your life. And, as you become increasingly self-reliant, you will experience new, exciting levels of freedom and independence to do what you want to do and be who you want to be.

Most of all, if you look in the right places you will discover mature, meaningful love and trusting relationships that provide unbounded fulfillment. And, if you wait until you can truly appreciate the comfort of marriage and unequaled joys of raising a family, there will be endless moments of profound pride and satisfaction that make your school years seem like kid stuff.

Michael Josephson

Unlimited Visibility: Pursue Grand Goals

Not long ago I had the privilege of delivering a commencement address to graduates of the Pepperdine University School of Law. The setting was incredible — a grassy plateau carved into the Malibu hills. The graduates and their families faced a podium framed by a vista of the coastline and the Pacific Ocean as deep into the horizon as you could see. Their view was literally unlimited.

My remarks were prepared ahead of time, and I didn't have the courage or confidence to change them to reflect the marvelous metaphor suggested by this unusual setting. Yet as I drove home, I wondered about the vision these graduates had for their lives.

I suspect that for a great many, the impending bar exam, worries about getting a job and the need to repay student loans obstruct any grand vision of the future. Like many who traverse years of education to earn a professional degree, I suspect most law school graduates see their lives in increments defined by successive challenges and goals — getting into law school, graduating, passing the bar, getting a job, becoming a partner. The hope is that each new hard-earned milestone will take them closer to prosperity, status and independence.

There's certainly nothing wrong with this progression, but I can't help wondering whether many of these highly competent men and women would make different choices along the way, lead different lives, if they looked beyond today's obstructions to see their limitless potential.

Yes, that potential includes the possibility of being fabulously rich and powerful. But it also includes the possibility of being enormously important as measured by lives touched.

What a challenge it is to consider our lives in terms of worthiness rather than worth, and significance rather than success.

So don't sell yourself short. Pursue grand goals.

Michael Josephson

The Road to Freedom and Independence

Someone once said that the subtle line between childhood and adulthood is crossed when we move from saying "It got lost" to "I lost it." Indeed, the willingness to accept responsibility for what we do and what we fail or refuse to do is a crucial sign of emotional and moral maturity as well as integrity. That's why responsibility is one of the pillars of good character.

As the well-known song from the musical *Peter Pan*, "I Won't Grow Up," suggests, one aspect of responsibility involves burdensome obligations that some would like to avoid.

Among the most important landmarks of maturity are acceptance of the fact that we are accountable for how we respond to the demands and opportunities of life and recognition that the benefits of being responsible greatly outweigh the disadvantages. Those who never grow up may always look at carrying their own weight, standing on their own two feet, preparing and setting goals, and exercising the discipline and self-control to reach those goals as burdens to be avoided. However, an inescapable fact of life is that being responsible is the surest road to trust, and trust is the surest road to freedom and independence. To be thought of as someone who can be depended on is a tremendous asset in personal and business relationships.

What's more, it's tremendously empowering to learn that within the notion of responsibility is the vital insight that we all have the power to control our actions and attitudes and that we all can change our lives by changing our attitudes.

Character in Family and Relationships

Live so that when your children think of fairness and integrity, they think of you.

H. Jackson Brown, Jr.

You Can't Fly Without Strong Wings

A young mother was fascinated watching a butterfly emerging from its cocoon, but she became concerned as she watched it struggle mightily trying to escape through a tiny opening at the top. The butterfly's effort widened the opening but not enough, and after awhile it stopped, exhausted and overwhelmed by the task.

The mother felt certain that the butterfly would never make it without help, so she delicately cut a small slit to enlarge the escape hole. When the butterfly renewed its struggle it was able to wriggle out of the cocoon easily. But something was wrong; although it escaped, its wings were shriveled and frail. The butterfly was no longer confined in the cocoon, but without strong wings it could never be free.

What happened was that the well-meaning intervention actually sentenced the butterfly to a short and unhappy life. You see, forcing the butterfly to squeeze through a small opening in the cocoon is nature's way of assuring that blood from the creature's body is pushed into its wings. Without that blood the wings were useless.

Childhood, too, is a sort of cocoon. If a healthy, mature adult is to emerge there must be some struggle. Love and tenderness are important, but children can't become adults with character unless they learn to be self-reliant.

Good parents always provide love and moral support, but they also teach their children strategies and give them tools to deal with their own problems. Overprotective parents who insist on solving all problems and removing all obstacles do more damage than good.

Children must be allowed to learn from their mistakes and pay the price for their own bad judgments. Parents who are always willing to bail their children out of trouble and shield them from the consequences of their choices do no one any favors. Remember, you can't fly without strong wings.

Michael Josephson

A Letter From Dad on Graduation Day

When my son Justin graduated high school and college I congratulated him and hugged him with great pride, but I let the graduation speakers send him forth with their valedictory advice. The last thing he wanted or needed from me, I thought, was another lecture on life. But there were things I wanted to say.

So, though they are a long way off, I'm preparing myself for the graduations of his four younger sisters and I decided to write a letter that they can keep and hopefully refer to when they are more receptive. Here's part of that letter:

"It's normal for you to be filled with conflicting emotions, including sadness, for what you are leaving behind, and a mixture of excitement and apprehension for what's in front of you. It's wise to be cautious but don't be frightened. You have all the tools you need to be happy and successful.

"It's important to set goals, but remember it's likely that your career and your personal life will take unexpected turns. How you cope with these unplanned ups and downs will both shape and reveal your character. But more importantly, it will determine the quality of your life.

"Be careful not to let either your successes or failures get to your head. Take them in stride, learn from them, build on them, but remember that almost nothing is as good or as bad as it first appears.

"Be strong and you will overcome every disappointment and personal tragedy. Persist with the confidence that no feeling of pain, frustration or despair can withstand the sustained power of your will to be happy.

"And as you begin your working life, keep your perspective about what's important. Don't lose sight of who you are and who you want to be. Don't get caught up in the gamesmanship of your job or measure your value in terms of your earnings or position or the approval of others.

— continued on next page —

Michael Josephson

"Don't allow yourself to be so self-absorbed and calculating that you begin to think that everything that could possibly advance or hinder your career is vital and that nothing else is of equal importance.

"In fact, the importance of almost every crisis you face in your working life will shrink with the passage of time. It's the way you deal with your personal life and relationships that will have the most enduring impact.

"Finally, don't put a price tag on the importance of people or neglect or hurt those who care about you. Without someone to share them with, your achievements will be short-lived like the beauty of cut flowers.

"So, go forth and enjoy the great feast ahead."

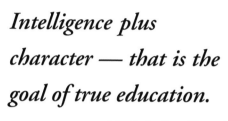

Intelligence plus character — that is the goal of true education.

Martin Luther King, Jr.

The Gap Between What We Say and What We Do

Ask parents, "What's the most important thing in your life?" and most will say, "My family." Ask the spouses and children of especially hardworking parents and many will say, "His work," "Her career" or "Money." While the overworked parent says that long hours and travel are sacrifices made for the family, most children would trade the financial benefits just to have mom or dad more available — not only physically, but emotionally.

As a workaholic myself I know that one consequence of being preoccupied with work is that it often makes us inattentive, impatient and unappreciative of the small things that build quality relationships. So we often find a wide gap between what we say we value and what we actually value as demonstrated by the choices we make. This gap is often a major source of personal conflict and deep resentments.

In some cases, the problem is an analytical one — our highest priority really is the family, but we seriously miscalculate what our families want and need the most. It's often easy to overweigh the long-term importance of the things that money can buy and discount the value of the things that can be acquired or given only with the investment of time — intimacy, shared joys, understanding, moral support and counsel.

In other cases, the problem is self-delusion. The truth is that some people really place a higher value on their work and what it brings them in terms of personal satisfaction or financial rewards, but they don't want to admit it, even to themselves. Some parents don't really like home life that much and they use their work as a hideout. Others are fortunate enough to have really challenging and rewarding jobs that take so much time and energy that there isn't too much left for family. Either way, they are making trade-offs with lifelong consequences that they may come to regret. Rarely does anyone on his or her deathbed say, "I wish I spent more time at the office."

Sweet Adversity

No one wants pain, troubles or hardship but it's absolutely inevitable that we all will have plenty of each. And they won't always come in forms we prefer, doses we think are manageable or at times of our choosing. Adversity is never welcome, but it is not necessarily our enemy.

In fact, our character, more than anything else, will determine the quality of our lives, and our character will be shaped by how we deal with adversities — from everyday dislikes, difficulties and disappointments to deaths and disasters.

Shakespeare said, "Sweet are the uses of adversity / Which, like the toad, ugly and venomous, / Wears yet a precious jewel in his head." Adversity's precious jewel is cut by confidence and competence, forged in a process of confronting and overcoming difficulties.

The path to achievement and fulfillment often passes through the aggravations and hazards of life's thorny underbrush. Once we learn that adversities are simply obstacles, not prisons, we can develop the courage, patience, perseverance and will to solve problems we cannot avoid and bear pains we cannot relieve.

As the blade is sharpened by a harder stone, so too character is strengthened through struggle and striving. Nietzsche put it another way: "What doesn't destroy me makes me stronger."

This poem by an unknown author reminds us that what we need is not always what we want:

> *I asked for Strength*
> *And God gave me Difficulties to make me strong.*
> *I asked for Wisdom*
> *And God gave me Problems to solve.*
> *I asked for Prosperity*
> *And God gave me Brain and Brawn to work.*
> *I asked for Courage*
> *And God gave me Danger to overcome.*
> *I asked for Love*
> *And God gave me Troubled People to help.*
> *I asked for Favor*
> *And God gave me Opportunities.*
> *I got nothing I wanted.*
> *But I received everything I needed.*

Michael Josephson

Words of Appreciation

The students at Sandy's high school were badly shaken by the news that a classmate had committed suicide. He left a note saying, "It's hard to live when nobody cares if you die." Realizing this was both a traumatic event that needed to be confronted and a teachable moment, Sandy's teacher talked about the importance of feeling valued and he gave an assignment. "Imagine," he said, "that someone who has meant a lot to you is dying. Write a note to tell that person how much you appreciate him or her."

Sandy, who had a rocky relationship with her mother, was especially moved by the assignment. She wrote a note to her mom saying: "We've had some rough times and I know I haven't been a very good daughter. I haven't been all that you wanted me to be or all that I wanted to be and I sometimes take it out on you. But I know you love me and that I'm lucky to have you in my life. You are the best person I've ever known. Thanks for not giving up on me."

When Sandy got home, she could see her mother was crying and vulnerable so she put her note on her mom's pillow where she would find it before she went to sleep and could read it in private.

When Sandy went to bed, she was surprised to find an envelope under *her* pillow. It was a note from her mom. "My dearest daughter," it said, "I know I have not been the kind of mother you wanted and deserved. I am so sorry. Being your mother was the best and most important thing in my life. But I can't bear this feeling of failure anymore. Forgive me."

Fearing that her mother was going to take her life, Sandy rushed into her mom's room to find her on the bed sobbing. She had Sandy's note in her hand. Sandy grabbed her mother and hugged her. "Don't leave me, Mom. I need you. Everything is going to get better," she cried. Her mom took Sandy's face in her hands and said, "I know."

Baloney Sandwich Relationships

Jason, a construction worker who brought his lunch to work, opened up his bag and flew into a rage. "I can't believe it! Baloney again. I hate baloney." Trying to calm him down, a coworker said, "If you hate baloney so much, just ask your wife to make you something else." Jason replied, "That won't work. I make my own lunches."

There are lots of people in this world who make their own baloney sandwiches and then act as victims of their own choices. It's like the audacious murderer who killed his parents and then asked the court for mercy since he was an orphan.

The baloney sandwich is a metaphor for things we do to ourselves that we don't take responsibility for.

Take personal relationships, for example. Don't you know people who continually get themselves involved in baloney sandwich relationships? Sometimes physical attraction is too strong a lure, sometimes loneliness is too much to bear, and sometimes they have a rescue mentality. But whatever the attraction, lots of intelligent men and women disable their good sense and high standards and ignore their experience by repeatedly getting involved with people who are bad for them.

If you have had more than one unsuccessful relationship with people who share the same defect, spot the pattern and break it. There's an old saying: "When you're in a hole, stop digging." In other words, assess your situation and take charge of your life. Don't dig in; climb out.

All Mothers Aren't Perfect

Mothers. What class of people has been more glorified or vilified? On the one hand, we are frequently confronted with an idealized image of the saintly, white-haired mother with tender hands callused from work. She is the embodiment of the most beneficent human qualities: nurturing, loving, devoted and wise.

The luckiest of us have had mothers who are worthy of the appreciation. Abraham Lincoln expressed this when he said: "All that I am or hope to be, I owe to my angel mother." Henry Ward Beecher spoke of the huge impact that mothers can have on the values, ambition and self-concept of their children when he said, "The mother's heart is the child's schoolroom." Treasure the gift she is and the gifts she gave you.

But the idea that we are what our mothers made of us can also make mothers a scapegoat for our insecurities and failures. Today, children are as likely to denounce their mothers' faults as glorify their virtues. And, to be fair, some mothers fall far short of the noble ideal.

Let's face it. Some mothers are consistently wonderful, some are predominantly hurtful, and most are a mixed bag. Surely, all mothers are not reflexively affirming. When a national magazine described her Nobel Prize-winning son as "the world's smartest man," the prize winner's mom told a reporter, "If that's the world's smartest man, God help us." Some mothers are never satisfied. Some nag. Some are controlling and judgmental.

Okay, so all mothers aren't perfect. Women don't lose their normal human flaws or become wise simply because they become mothers. Still, being a parent does bring the best out of most people and even less than perfect parents make huge sacrifices on behalf of their children. The best of mothers has made mistakes and the worst has provided moments of comfort and joy.

Discover and prize the best in your mother. Love her for what she is and for the life she gave you. There is no closer bond.

Judging Our Parents, Judging Our Kids

Think of three good things you remember most about your father. For me, I remember, first, that my dad loved me and he always showed it, even with wet kisses that made me cringe. Second, when I was cut from a baseball team as a too-small 11-year-old, he started a new team. I couldn't hit but I was walked a lot, so my dad made the "on base average" the most important statistic on our team. Finally, I remember his relentless insistence that if I wanted something badly enough I could get it. His mantra: "If there's a will there's a way. If there's not, there's an alibi."

He was an exceptionally good dad — affectionate, involved, creative and very smart. But he wasn't a perfect person. He yelled too much. And when he wanted something, he could be controlling and manipulative. In business, he often displayed a New York street morality that fell short of my ideal. I used to think it was disloyal or ungrateful even to think such thoughts, but now that he's been gone for 20 years, it's easier to see and accept him as a full-dimensional man with virtues and flaws like everyone else.

While I always loved my dad, I was often ungenerously judgmental about his shortcomings. But as I got older and was able to compare him to fathers who were abusive, neglectful or even indifferent to their children I realized how truly lucky I was. I so wish I appreciated him more when he was with me.

It's a shame and a pity that so many kids judge their parents too harshly, thinking most often about their biggest faults and worst acts.

Unfortunately, some parents are equally hard on their kids. When parents or children think the relationship gives them a right to demand perfection, they take every shortcoming personally and torment each other. But instead of getting perfection from these unreasonable expectations, we get emotional scars and bitter resentments.

— *continued on next page* —

Michael Josephson

How much wiser it is to be generous about those we know best and let our thoughts be filtered through their best attributes and our warmest memories.

If it's not too late, change your attitude about your parents or kids and you will change their lives.

Parents can plant magic in a child's mind through certain words spoken with some thrilling quality of voice, some uplift of the heart and spirit.

Robert MacNeil

I Love Being a Dad

When I wrote the original version of this commentary, it was very late and I was under lots of pressure. A messenger was scheduled to pick up a tape of my essay in a few hours and I was still struggling for a topic. Finally I realized that the things keeping me from writing were what I should write about: the woes and wonders of being a father of four young daughters.

The evening started with special alone time with Mataya, who had just turned three. She jumped on the "big bed" like a trampoline and I tackled and tickled her until she giggled surrender. As her mother took her away for a bath, her then four-and-a-half-year-old sister, Carissa, came home from a play date. She was tired and said she had "growing pains," so I rubbed her legs until our bedtime ritual began. I took the two little ones and my wife took the two bigger ones. I put on their pajamas and night-time diapers and told them stories until they fell asleep.

Just as I thought I was through, Abrielle retrieved me to say she didn't ever want to go to school again. She had a hard day in kindergarten. Her best friend told other girls that Abrielle couldn't read chapter books yet. This was true, but hardly anyone in her kindergarten class could. Still, my daughter was too ashamed to face the other kids. Fortunately, Samara, her then seven-year-old sister, convinced her that lots of kids liked her — they actually went through the names of everyone in her class. I cuddled Aby and got her to sleep with a story about puppets. Then it was Samara's turn. We talked for a half hour before she conked out.

It was 1:30 a.m. when I finally finished answering my e-mails and was just directing my attention to the radio commentary. Mataya sleepwalked into my office and silently raised her arms, sign language for "hold me." I picked her up hugged her and carried her back to bed, got her a new bottle of apple juice and within 10 minutes I was back at my computer.

— *continued on next page* —

Then Abrielle appeared. She had a bad dream and didn't want to go back to her bed. Feeling desperate, I let her make a bed of pillows on the floor and she fell asleep at my feet. The stress was mounting when Carissa entered with the declaration: "I'm soaking wet." She needed to be changed and she wanted a "warm T-shirt" (the one I was wearing). I stripped off my shirt, put on a new diaper and carried her into the "big bed" to sleep next to her mommy so I could get back to work.

It was nearly 3:00 a.m. when I returned to my desk feeling some resentment that my children were keeping me from my work. Then it struck me: They are my work! What's more, I love it.

I finally realized that I was in the middle of a glorious fathering feast and that I had better savor every moment. And once I realized that, the commentary just wrote itself.

The words that a father speaks to his children in the privacy of the home are not heard by the world, but, as in whispering galleries, they are clearly heard at the end, and by posterity.

Jean Paul Richter

A Father Can't Be a Best Friend

I t's common for parents to want to be best friends to their children, and many children want their parents to be more like friends than guardians. A few years ago, a man named Sergio Ferreira posted on the **CHARACTER COUNTS!** website (www.charactercounts.org) a letter to his teenage son explaining why he chose a different path. I've paraphrased the letter for brevity but the thoughts are his.

"When I was a teenager," he wrote, "I wished . . . my dad could be my best friend. However, it wasn't until [I became a father that] I understood . . . that a father who tries to be a best friend can't be a real father. . . .

"Being a friend is optional but being a father is a moral obligation," Mr. Ferreira added. "As your father, I must protect you physically and emotionally, give you support and encouragement, guide you and always set a good example. But more importantly, I'm responsible for your moral development. It's my God-given mission to instill in you ethical and moral values to help you become more responsible, self-sufficient and compassionate, and to encourage you to strive to be a better son, brother and husband and, above all, a better human being before God.

"Some day you'll understand completely the . . . meaning of this letter. On that day, you and I will start to develop a unique and profound bond. When that day comes, you'll never forget it, for it will be one of the happiest days of your life. On that day, you'll receive [as I once did] a beautiful blessing and an extraordinary responsibility. It will be the day when you hold in your arms your first child. From that moment on you'll also understand that more important than being your child's friend, it is to be a real father."

In a world looking for one-minute managers and one-week diets, Mr. Ferreira sought to teach his son and us an important lesson about the responsibility of parenthood. There are no shortcuts. It takes perseverance, constancy and more than a little hope and faith to be a good dad or mom. It takes character.

"Please Don't Go, Daddy"

I remember the day I told my daughter Samara (who was then five) that I was going on a trip for one night. "Please don't go, Daddy," she begged. When I wouldn't agree to stay, she threw an all-out tantrum. I knew that was the risk when I told her. I could have said nothing and let her mother explain my absence, or I could have pretended to give in by saying that "I'd see" if I could get out of it. Well, actually I couldn't. You see, I made a decision long before that I wanted to establish relationships of unquestioned trust with my children. And I knew that even well-intentioned lies, deceptions and broken promises could be land mines to trust.

When she calmed down she took a new tack. "Take me with you." When this didn't work she came up with her final offer: "Then I want you to wear this tie." And she got a tie she had given me for Father's Day. It was a special tie, one that she'd drawn pictures on.

When I dressed for my trip, I thought of putting the tie in my briefcase and wearing one more appropriate. But a promise is a promise, so I wore the tie. During my talk, I told the tie story in the context of trust, pointing out that while I was certain my daughter would never know if I wore the tie or not, trust is too precious to take chances with.

When I returned the next afternoon wearing the same clothes I went straight to my office. Later, my wife showed up in a surprise visit with all four kids. She had never done that before. When Samara saw I was wearing the tie, she beamed and gave me a huge hug. I was so glad I kept my promise.

If You Broke It, at Least Try to Fix It

When former president Jimmy Carter was 70 years old he wrote this poem about his father:

> *This is a pain I mostly hide,*
> *but ties of blood, or seed endure,*
> *and even now I feel inside*
> *the hunger for his outstretched hand,*
> *a man's embrace to take me in,*
> *the need for just a word of praise.*

Isn't it extraordinary that even after a life of monumental achievements, Mr. Carter still feels pain when he thinks of his father, who either could not feel, or would not express, love and approval? Unfortunately, there are lots of people in Mr. Carter's shoes, left with bitter feelings and enduring wounds inflicted by abusive, neglectful or simply careless parents. Parental malpractice ranges from the morally criminal acts of physical and verbal abuse to abandonment, emotional coldness, neglect, alcoholism and exploitative selfishness.

Yet not all bad parents are bad people. Caring parents can unintentionally injure children through excessive harshness or permissiveness, or through well-intended criticism and advice that comes out as relentless disapproval or oppressive negativity. Kids not only need to know they're loved; they need to feel worthy of our love. They need to be valued not simply because they're ours, but because of who they are.

Because the parent-child relationship is of lifelong importance, it deserves special attentiveness and requires servicing. Making things better can be particularly difficult when grown children have become parental abusers themselves. What's more, those who feel wronged may not be ready to forgive. Still others may be like Jimmy Carter, starving for special recognition and approval.

Either way, it's never too late to try to fix whatever is broken. Consider expressing caring, pride and approval more lavishly and more often.

— continued on next page —

Michael Josephson

Be less critical, more helpful and less controlling. Set aside your need to be right; be less self-righteous and more respectful toward the people you love. Be sincerely accountable and genuinely apologize even if whatever you do may not be enough.

It's not always possible to fix things that are broken, but it's worth a try.

Success consists of getting up just one more time than you fall.

Oliver Goldsmith

The Blue Stone and the White Lie

I've talked before about the importance I attach to maintaining a high level of trust with my children and how I regard even well-intentioned lies and deceptions as land mines. Still, I must admit that I'm not an absolutist, and that there are circumstances where a lie may be morally justified. I faced this choice a few years ago when my then four-year-old daughter Abrielle came screaming down the hall. Her then five-year-old sister Samara was right behind her, equally terrified. "I swallowed a stone. I don't want to die," Abrielle cried in terror. Samara sobbed, "I don't want Aby to die."

I immediately determined that nothing was obstructing Abrielle's throat and that she was breathing normally, but she was still in a panic. "It's OK, Sweetheart. You're not going to die," I said. She thought I didn't understand. "But I swallowed a stone!"

I quickly established that she had swallowed a small polished stone — "a blue one" she kept emphasizing, as if it were deadly rat poison. She was convinced she was going to die because her babysitter, in order to discourage her from putting foreign objects in her mouth, told Aby that she could die if she swallowed something.

I assured her she was in no danger. I told her that the stone would come out in the morning when she went "poo-poo." She ran to the toilet. "I want it out now!" she screamed. She was pushing so hard it looked like a blood vessel would burst. The truth wasn't working. So I lied. I traded truth to ease her pain.

"Wait a minute," I said and I ran to get a spoonful of maple syrup. "Here, swallow this syrup. It will melt the stone."

"Will it be gone?" she said.

"Absolutely," I replied. She took the spoonful of syrup, and her face relaxed immediately. In a moment she announced triumphantly: "Daddy melted the stone. I'm not going to die." I was her hero, and I loved it.

— *continued on next page* —

Michael Josephson

Still, it bothered me. Perhaps I shouldn't have thought twice about this little deception, but I know how fragile trust is, and how easy it is to rationalize ethical shortcuts under pressure. I also didn't want her to think that maple syrup really can melt stones. So later I told her the truth and why I made up the story. She just hugged me and said, "That's OK, Daddy. I know you love me."

> *What wisdom can you find that is greater than kindness?*

Jean-Jacques Rousseau

What Children Owe Their Parents

I t's well known that parents can inflict lasting emotional pain on their children. Parenting is an awesome moral responsibility that both tests and reveals our character. But so is being a good child. Just as children need encouragement and approval from parents, moms and dads also want, deserve and need validation from their kids.

Yes, it's natural for maturing children to become preoccupied with their own lives and with liberating themselves from the physical, psychic and financial control of their parents. And good parents support emerging needs for independence. But none of this frees children from the basic responsibilities of kindness, courtesy, respect and gratitude.

Self-absorbed youngsters — teens and young adults — often convince themselves that they're too busy or poor to be attentive to parental emotional needs, or even common courtesies. So they just don't get around to making thoughtful phone calls or buying symbolic birthday, anniversary and holiday gifts. (With parents, it really is the thought that counts.) And because their parents forgive them, they think what they did, or didn't do, was OK. Well, it isn't.

Good parents — often the ones easiest to hurt — don't change their lives in thousands of ways when they have children in order to earn their children's gratitude. But their parental devotion makes their children's thoughtlessness more hurtful. King Lear in a moment of despair utters an age-old truth: "How sharper than a serpent's tooth it is to have a thankless child."

Children of all ages have an enormous power to cause happiness or hurt. Deciding to share good news can give a parent a source of pride and joy, while choosing to ignore, demean or shut out a parent can cause enduring distress, even misery. Children of character don't look for excuses. They make choices that honor and uplift their parents.

Michael Josephson

The Nature of Character and Ethics

Fame is a vapor, popularity an accident, riches take wing and only character endures.

Horace Greeley

We Shape Our Own Character

There's no doubt that our character has a profound effect on our future. What we must remember, however, is not merely how powerful character is in influencing our destiny, but how powerful we are in shaping our own character and, therefore, our own destiny. Character may determine our fate, but character is not determined by fate.

It's a common mistake to think of character as something that is fully formed and fixed very early in life. It calls to mind old maxims like "A leopard can't change its spots" and "You can't teach an old dog new tricks." This "etched in stone" perspective is supported by a great deal of modern psychology emphasizing self-acceptance. Like Popeye says, "I am what I am." The message is: "I'm done. Don't expect me to be more, better or different."

These views of character totally undervalue the lifelong potential for growth that comes with the power of reflection and choice. How depressing it would be to believe that we really couldn't get better, that with dedication and effort, we couldn't become more honest, respectful, responsible or caring.

There are so many things in life we can't control — whether we're beautiful or smart, whether we had good parents or bad, whether we grew up with affirmation or negation or with affluence or poverty. And though these circumstances of our lives surely influence our values and experiences, they do not control them. People of good and bad character come from all sorts of circumstances.

It's uplifting to remember that nothing but moral willpower is needed to make us better. No, it isn't easy. But if we strive to become more aware of the habits of heart and mind that drive our conduct, we can begin to place new emphasis on our higher values and become what we want our children to think we are.

The Self-Portrait Called Character

I was on a radio show talking about what I called the growing hole in our moral ozone when Steve called to chastise my naiveté. He cheated to get into college, he said. He cheated in college to get a job. And now, he occasionally cheats on his job to get ahead. Cheating is part of our culture. So, rather than urge parents to teach kids to be honest, he claimed, I ought to urge parents to teach their kids how to cheat.

Tempting logic. In fact, lots of people cheat, and most of them get away with it. Why should a rational person be ethical? This age-old question is at the core of our personal philosophy of life and the concept we have of our selves.

To those who see their lives and derive their happiness purely in terms of material acquisitions, an unethical life is a viable alternative. If Steve is smart enough to avoid all the traps and pitfalls of this sort of life and never get caught — an unlikely scenario — he may even achieve a sort of happiness.

But those who care about other things — about relationships, about peace of mind, about living a worthy life and being admired and remembered for it — know that people like Steve are a bit pathetic.

We paint the self-portrait that we call our character by our actions. We can choose to paint that portrait in the pale watercolors of shallow successes and short-lived pleasures, or in the deep, rich oils of love, honor and reverence for our human potential.

The happiest people I know are those who find purpose, meaning and self-respect in pursuing a vision of a good life, guided and measured by enduring moral virtues. They realize it's demeaning and self-defeating to get caught up in the daily quest for profit or advantage. People like Steve have no idea the price they're paying for the little they're getting.

Remember, the importance of what you do goes well beyond what it gets you; it determines who you are. And who you are is infinitely more important than what you have.

Bridging the Gap Between the Is and the Ought

During a workshop for high-level executives, it became clear that there was widespread dissatisfaction about the ethical state of their industry. The participants wanted everyone to live up to higher standards. That is, until we got down to specific situations where scrupulous truth-telling, promise-keeping and good-faith compliance would require changes that could negatively affect the bottom line or become competitive disadvantages.

It seems that everyone is for ethics in the abstract.

It's not uncommon to hear someone condemn situational ethics and moral relativism one moment, only to defend some deceptive, misleading or otherwise improper professional practice the next. Most people want to do their jobs with complete integrity but, despite popular rhetoric that good ethics is good business, many don't seem to believe it. Or they're just not willing to pay the cost.

Let's face it. Ethics can be quite constraining, especially in a business context. Consequently, lofty ideas about morality and virtue often give way to more pragmatic standards of decision making, involving factors such as what it takes to win, what our competitors are doing, and what we're likely to get away with. "Do what's right" becomes "Do what works."

The hard thing is to live up to our moral aspirations when there is a wide gap between the "is" — what people are actually doing — and the "ought" — what people should be doing based on moral principles. People of character know that ethics is not about the way things are. It's about the way they ought to be.

Ethical standards are prescriptive, not descriptive. They tell us how we should behave. And they're not merely suggestions. They're ground rules.

64

The Myth of Nonjudgmentalness

As a product of the '60s, I graduated college with one strong moral conviction: "It's wrong to be judgmental." After all, in a world where some cultures eat dogs, others eat snails and still others eat their enemies, who am I to judge? I was an ethical relativist, convinced that ideas of ethics and morality simply reflect social conventions or personal opinions. Of course, this was pretty convenient. Relativism made no demands on me, and it instructed me to refrain from making demands on others. It's what Ayn Rand called an exchange of moral blank checks: "I won't judge you if you don't judge me."

All this changed when I became a father. If I allowed my moral agnosticism to make me so unsure about ethical values that I couldn't say that some things are right and some things are wrong, what guidance could I give my children on matters like lying, cheating, violence and racism?

I came to realize nonjudgmentalness is a myth. Refusing to judge is itself the result of the judgment that there are no valid criteria for right and wrong. On reflection, it seemed clear to me that my firm conviction that Mahatma Gandhi led a better, more worthy life than Adolf Hitler was more than just personal opinion.

I'm still put off by the image of a self-righteous finger-wagging moralist imposing all his personal values on others. But the other extreme can be just as bad. In the end, it's simply irresponsible to treat kindness and cruelty, altruism and selfishness, justice and injustice as moral equivalents. Now I believe that there is a handful of enduring, universal moral truths and I think they're embodied in what I call the "Six Pillars of Character" — trustworthiness, respect, responsibility, fairness, caring and good citizenship.

The Golden Rule as the Road to Honor

Five hundred years before the birth of Christ, Confucius was asked, "Is there one word which may serve as a rule of practice for all one's life?" He answered, "Reciprocity. What you do not want done to yourself, do not do to others." This basic principle, now called the Golden Rule, can be found in every major religion and philosophy.

Many people evoke one version or another of this rule, but it's often misused. You see, the Golden Rule is not primarily a rule of enlightened self-interest. Sure, people are more likely to be nice to you if you're nice to them, but the moral center of this principle is lost if you simply view it as a rule of exchange: do unto others so they will do unto you. Or: do unto others as they have done unto you. Let alone: do unto others before they do unto you.

The core of the Golden Rule is a moral obligation to treat others ethically for their sake, not ours, even if it's better than the way they treat us. So we should be honest to liars, fair to the unjust and kind to people who are cruel. Why? Not because it's advantageous, but because it's right. And because the way I treat others is about who I am, not who they are. It's like the man who broke off an argument that descended to name-calling, saying, "Sir, I will treat you as a gentleman, not because you are one, but because I am one."

Sure, if we commit to always treating others the way we want to be treated, we'll be taken advantage of occasionally. But that's also true of those who are always trying to outsmart their neighbors.

Michael Josephson

Parenting, Teaching and Coaching Character

The best way to teach morality is to make it a habit with children.

Aristotle

Modeling and Markers

Jaren was working on a school project with an impressive set of colored markers. His dad asked where they came from. "I took them from school," Jaren said.

"Are you allowed to do that?"

"Not really, but I'll return them tomorrow."

Taken aback, his father said, "I can't believe you'd do that. It's against everything I ever taught you. If you needed them so badly, why didn't you tell me? I would have taken them from the office." Dad meant well, but the values he conveyed are not likely to produce good character.

Just as a mighty tree cannot live without healthy roots, good character requires good values. We should teach, enforce and advocate positive values like honesty and responsibility, but modeling — what we say and do in front of children — is the most influential way parents, teachers and coaches teach character. And because children are much more likely to do as we do than as we say, it's important to think about the values we may be teaching through our actions. What's more, it's not necessarily our self-conscious efforts to demonstrate virtue that have the most impact. Rather, it's about how we behave when we're off-guard, when we think no one is looking.

Children watch how we cope with stress, anger and good fortune. They notice whether we're accountable or make up excuses, whether we deal with or avoid our problems. Everything we say and do sends a message. So if you want to help your children build the type of character you're proud of, always act as if your children are watching. And you know what? They are.

Michael Josephson

Parents Are
Teachers First

I was at a meeting when John Wooden, the legendary UCLA basketball coach, was asked about his decision to retire. When he talked about "the last game I ever taught," he was asked about this unusual phrasing. He said simply that a coach is first and foremost a teacher who should not only improve his players' athletic skills but help them become better people. In fact, as scores of former players will attest, John Wooden was a superb teacher. His teams won 10 national titles. But his most lasting influence is reflected in the values he instilled in his players, not the championships they won.

Henry Adams observed that teachers affect all eternity. As those who are taught teach others, the teacher's influence and impact grows. Sadly, the way we select and reward schoolteachers and coaches shows how much we undervalue their crucial role in shaping the character and destiny of our children.

But even worse, we tend to forget that the first and by far the most important teachers are those engaged in parenting. Good childrearing involves more than providing food, shelter and education. It involves instilling good values and habits. It involves teaching right from wrong and how to make good decisions that are both effective and ethical.

Yes, it's important to help kids become smart and competent, but as Teddy Roosevelt said, "To educate a person in the mind but not the morals is to educate a menace to society." Parents need to be attentive and dedicated to assuring that their children have the tools to lead truly good lives, lives with purpose and meaning and value. That means we need to teach, enforce, advocate and model the best we want our children to be.

Character Building Requires Teamwork

All parents, and most teachers and coaches, want to help youngsters develop good character. What's more, most believe that they're already doing a pretty good job. And some are. But given the enormous importance and complexity of developing character, I think we've got to be more purposeful and proficient. Good is not enough. We need a more coherent strategy.

That's why I believe so deeply in the CHARACTER COUNTS! program, built on a small list of character traits called the "Six Pillars of Character": trustworthiness, respect, responsibility, fairness, caring and citizenship. Since the six words lend themselves to the acronym "TRRFCC," we tell youngsters that character is terrific.

Serious and comprehensive attempts to instill or strengthen these virtues involve thoughtful efforts to increase a youngster's ethical consciousness (awareness of the moral implications of actions), ethical commitment (the desire and willpower to do the right thing) and ethical competence (the ability to foresee potential consequences and devise ethical alternatives).

The CHARACTER COUNTS! strategy is built on the word "TEAM," another acronym. The T stands for "teach," E for "enforce," A for "advocate" and M for "model."

The first step in effective character building is to teach young people about the nature and importance of good character by defining, illustrating and demanding the traits embodied in the Six Pillars of Character.

Next, we have to enforce the principles by consistently imposing fair, firm and timely consequences on conduct that departs from these moral norms.

Third, in a world emerging from the dominance of "whatever works for you" values clarification strategies, we must boldly advocate

— continued on next page —

Michael Josephson

adherence to moral principles by exhorting, encouraging, and inspiring a belief that character really does count.

Finally, if we want to influence the values of children, we have to model ethical behavior ourselves in all we say and do.

It's not easy, but if we care about our kids and the world they are growing up in, we have no choice.

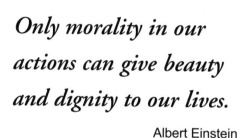

Only morality in our actions can give beauty and dignity to our lives.

Albert Einstein

Kids and Play-Doh

Peggy Adkins, a talented CHARACTER COUNTS! trainer, tells the story of when she and her family went to adopt a cat. Each member of the family was interviewed, and when the shelter finally gave them a cat, Peggy's family had to sign a document that listed 23 things to do and 17 things not to do to raise a happy, healthy cat. After one month, and then three months later, they received a call checking whether they were doing the 23 things they were supposed to do and refraining from the 17 things they were not supposed to do.

Peggy thought this was a wonderfully responsible way to handle cat adoptions but, as the mother of two adopted children, she couldn't help but marvel at the fact that she got better training and follow-up about her cat than her children. After all, raising happy, healthy and decent children is vastly more complicated and important than raising cats. Where's the instruction manual for parenting?

She makes her point emphatically by passing out pieces of fresh Play-Doh in different sizes and colors. She points out that no two pieces are exactly alike and that each piece can be molded into infinitely unique shapes. "Now," she says, "indent the clay slightly with your finger, touch it with your fingernail, and then press it against your bare arm and notice that every touch makes a mark. Press it against the Sunday comics and it will mirror the pictures. And if you roll the Play-Doh on the table it will pick up all kinds of little things, bits and particles that are awfully hard to remove."

This Play-Doh is like our children. Everything we do, everything we expose them to, makes an impression.

"I'm Better Than That"

Ron, a nine-year-old boy, was being raised by his mother who didn't know how to cope with his uncontrollable temper. She knew he was angry that his father had abandoned him, and she tried professional counseling, but nothing seemed to work. So she sent Ron to spend the summer on his grandparents' farm. When he came home he was a changed boy. His mom asked him what had happened.

Ron told her that every time he got mad or said anything unkind, Grandpa Hal made him go outside and hammer a big two-inch nail into a two-by-four. It was really hard and he wasn't allowed back until the nail was all the way in. After about 20 trips to the shed, he decided it was easier to control his temper than hammer in those nails.

"So," his mom said, "you hated the consequence so much you just changed?"

"Well," he answered, "that was part of it. After I had hit in all these nails and was behaving pretty well, Grandma Grace took me outside and made me pull out all the nails. That was just as hard. But when I was done she gave me this note that I've been carrying around."

The note said: "Pulling out nails is like saying you're sorry. But remember the holes you left in the board. You can't fix it by being sorry, but you can stop making new holes. Remember, every time you do something mean and nasty you are making a hole somewhere, in someone. That's what your Dad did to you. Please don't do that to anyone else. You are better than that."

"You know what, Mom," Ron said, "Grandma's right. I'm better than that."

Teachable Moments: Keep on Knocking

I'm a big believer in "teachable moments": the idea that we all experience moments when we are unusually receptive to learning something especially important about ourselves or how the world works. Like the summer I took a second job as a door-to-door salesman selling Fuller brushes. My mother had passed away a few months earlier, and I desperately wanted to earn enough money to have a photo of her turned into a painted portrait for my dad.

What I earned depended entirely on what I sold. There were no guarantees. Things went well at first, but then I hit a long bad streak. Hardly anyone was home, and those who were just weren't buying. Some people were outright rude. I was on the verge of quitting, but I couldn't stop thinking of something I knew my father would say to me if I gave up: "Where there's a will, there's a way. Where there's not, there's an alibi."

I always resented this simplistic nagging, but suddenly it hit home. I realized that every meaningful opportunity in life would stay behind closed doors, doors that would never open unless I knocked on them. If I couldn't muster the confidence and courage to knock on more doors despite the certainty of frustrating and unpleasant experiences, I would never make it.

I realized that if I persisted and kept a positive attitude despite unpleasant experiences, I'd eventually hit my average. The lesson: just keep on knocking. Sure enough, things got better and I ended up the top salesman in my region.

Much later in life, reflection on that summer taught me another valuable lesson. I was feeling discouraged about my inability to get my son to understand the importance of persistence and hard work when it hit me — it was another teachable moment. I realized that persistence in parenting is just as vital. Keep on knocking. Don't give up. Someday he'll get it.

Now, as I look at the portrait of my mom hanging next to my dad's in the lobby of the nonprofit Joseph and Edna Josephson Institute of Ethics named after them, I'm so glad I persisted, and so grateful I learned that an important part of character is to just keep on knocking.

Michael Josephson

"I Didn't Want the Janitor to Lose His Job"

Let there be no mistake — the primary responsibility for instilling good values and building character is with parents. This doesn't mean, however, that teachers and coaches don't have a critically important role. The unfortunate fact is that far too many kids are raised in morally impoverished settings that foster lying, cheating and disrespect. If we don't make an effort to give these children moral instruction, many of them will become predators.

I know outside-the-home character training works because of Jesse.

Jesse was in an alternative school because he had serious behavioral problems, including theft. About a month after his school incorporated explicit character-development strategies into the curriculum, Jesse found the janitor's keys and, to everyone's surprise, he voluntarily turned them in. When he was asked why, he said, "I didn't want the janitor to lose his job."

According to his teachers, Jesse would not have thought about the janitor just weeks before. Like a lot of young folks, he rarely thought about the likely consequences of his conduct.

What changed was that he was given a simple thinking tool that helped him see the way his choices could affect other people. Jesse was taught to identify "stakeholders" — all the people likely to be affected by a choice — and to think about how they might be affected.

For all Jesse's other flaws, he had decent instincts, and he didn't want to do something that would hurt the janitor. His teachers didn't teach him to care about others, but they did give him a way of thinking that unleashed the caring part of his nature.

Michael Josephson

"Thanks for Saving My Life"

Mario's job was to transport juveniles from a temporary detention facility to a longer-term detention center. One day he was transporting John, a 16-year-old charged with setting fire to his own house. Normally, Mario said nothing to his passengers and his passengers said nothing to him, and he liked it that way. But he heard John sobbing quietly in the back. He looked in his rearview mirror and saw a miserably unhappy child, and he thought of his own teenage son. Breaking his normal rule of silence, he said, "Son, it looks bad now but everything will get better."

John said, "It's not going to get better because I'm going to kill myself." Mario knew he could recommend psychiatric assistance as soon as he arrived at the detention center, but his fatherly impulses took over, and he spent the rest of the short 18-minute drive listening to John tell of his inability to do anything but disappoint his father. Mario tried to comfort the boy and again said, "Look, it may not feel like it now but I promise you, things will get better. Just hang in there." He then dropped the boy off, made a recommendation that he see a counselor at once and that was the end of it.

Two years later, Mario received an envelope addressed to "Mario, the transportation guy." Inside was a picture of John, with a girl, in front of a university building. The note said, "You were right. Things got better. Thanks for saving my life."

Mario framed the picture and the note together and mounted them on the dash of his transportation vehicle. Now, he talks to all the young men he transports.

Attributes and Attitudes of Character

What we have done for ourselves alone dies with us; what we have done for others and the world remains and is immortal.

Albert Pike

Kindness
Is Too Rare

A fellow named Max Ehrmann said: "I wish there were more kindly persons in the world. Our competitive life develops selfishness and unkindness. I am determined to do something about it. I cannot hope to convert many persons. To convert one person, I shall do well. I will begin with the person I know best — myself."

Once, this preoccupation with kindness would have seemed too soft to me. I valued kindness, but I placed a higher value on more manly virtues like truth, duty and justice. That's consistent with Harvard psychologist Carol Gilligan's contention that males tend to think of morality in terms of justice, while females tend to think of it in terms of caring.

While I still don't feel comfortable with the easy trade-offs some people make by perpetually sacrificing honesty to be nice, I have a greater and growing appreciation for simple kindness.

After noticing how many sour and outright nasty people we see in stores, in planes and on freeways, my wife Anne and I reflected on the many trips we made to the Arkansas Children's Hospital where our daughter Abrielle was being treated for a facial birthmark. At the hospital, in the hotel and even in the store where our daughter threw up, people were genuinely kind and considerate. We were under great stress and the kindness we were given made our burdens easier to carry.

Here, in Southern California, kindness and consideration are too rare. We use stress and competition as excuses, but the fact is we just don't let ourselves care enough to be nice. It sometimes takes self-control and conscious effort to be kind, but if we choose to feel and express compassion we give others a gift that makes our world.

"This Is My Dad, Joe Fleming"

Lori's father was 85 and in the last stages of cancer. His needs had gone beyond what she could provide at home. After checking him into the hospital she was distraught. Besides the senseless waiting and movement from one station to another, she saw an impersonal bureaucracy — full of competent but cold administrators, nurses and doctors who seemed either bothered, bored or burned out — transform her dad from Joe Fleming to case number 02-8341.

She couldn't bear thinking of entrusting the last days of her father's life to people who didn't seem to care. So she made it a point to get the names of every person she could who might work with her father, and she sent each of them a personally addressed envelope with a carnation attached. It contained pictures of her dad getting married, posing with his five children and standing in front of his shoe repair shop, along with this note:

"This is my dad, Joe Fleming, the father of five children who love him very much and already miss him. He's a very good man who fought for his country and worked hard for his family. I know you have many patients, but I have only one father. I only ask you to treat him as you would want others to treat your father. Thank you."

During every visit, she made a point to smile at and talk to everyone she could and say, "This is my dad, Joe Fleming." Within a week, Lori could tell by the way they looked at her father that he was no longer in the hands of strangers.

But she was surprised when a woman who she had not met came up to her and said, "Are you Joe Fleming's daughter?" When Lori said yes, the woman said, "I'm Jan, the administrator of the hospital. I just want to thank you for treating everyone so kindly and personally. We've never had someone who took the time to treat the staff as people. Thanks. You've transformed the atmosphere here. By the way, how's your dad doing?"

Gratitude and the Gift of Water

Long ago a young man crossing a desert came upon a spring of cool, crystal-clear water. The water was so delightful that he thought how much his grandfather Saul would love it, so he filled his leather canteen. After a two-day journey he presented the water to Saul, who immediately tasted it with an expression of great pleasure. He lavishly thanked his grandson, who went away with a happy heart.

Another grandson tasted the water and found it awful. The water had become stale because of the old leather container. Puzzled, the boy said, "Grandfather, the water was foul. Why did you pretend to like it?" Saul replied, "I wasn't pretending. It wasn't the water I tasted. I tasted the kindness of the heart that labored two days to bring it to me."

Saul's gracious reaction was itself a generous gift rewarding his grandson's thoughtfulness. And the lesson he taught the second grandson was still another gift: gratitude uplifts both the giver and receiver.

We understand this best when young children give us gifts. Whether it's a ceramic tray or a macaroni bracelet, we love it because we love our children and the idea behind the gift. Because we don't expect the gift to be anything we want, we can truly appreciate the spirit of the giver. Children, on the other hand, tend to value only the thing given.

We have to teach them, by words and example, that the thing given is simply the container for the love it embodies. It's as if each gift has a heart, a piece of the heart of the person who gave it. Gratitude is about appreciating the heart.

Dimensions of Respect

I received a letter from someone who wanted to challenge an assertion I had made to the effect that everyone should expect and demand to be treated with respect. She said her boss was abusive, dishonest and not worthy of respect. What right does he have, she asked, to demand respect?

First, we need to distinguish between three aspects of respect: what we think of others, how we treat others and how we demand to be treated.

In one sense, to respect a person means to hold that person in high esteem. This type of respect must be earned. No one is entitled to our esteem.

However, the ethical obligation of respect also governs how we act towards others. People of character treat others respectfully whether they deserve it or not. I'm reminded of the politician who refused to get in a name-calling match with an opponent. He said, "Sir, I will treat you like a gentleman, not because you are one, but because I am one." Sure, it's hard to treat people better than they treat us, but it's important to realize what's at stake. If we allow nasty, crude and selfish people to drag us down to their level, they set the tone of our lives and shape us in their image.

The final dimension of respect is self-respect. People with healthy self-respect have a strong sense of dignity and self-worth. They set boundaries and demand respectful treatment as an absolute condition of a relationship.

My listener's ethical dilemma is really not about how she treats her boss, but how she allows him to treat her. It often takes moral courage. But whether it's a bad relationship or a bad job, whether the abuser is a parent, spouse, child or boss, self-respect ought to cause us to terminate any relationship that subjects us to continuous disrespect.

Listen up!

R-E-S-P-E-C-T: Aretha Franklin taught us how to spell it. If we were lucky, our parents taught us what it means, and that it's a fundamental pillar of good character. Though we're not duty-bound to respect everyone in the sense that we hold them in high esteem, we are morally obligated to treat everyone with respect.

Often that means really listening to what others have to say. That means consciously hearing and actually considering what is being said. That's hard when we're not really interested or don't think much of the person talking or we are just waiting for our own turn to speak. The fact is that most of us don't listen very well, certainly not all the time and especially with the people closest to us. Kids are especially adept at tuning out their parents, but parents are equally skilled at ignoring or dismissing as foolish or irrelevant what their kids have to say.

The disrespectfulness of not listening is most apparent when we are being ignored or patronized by others. As when someone we are talking to rolls his eyes in a show of impatience or contempt, or fake interest is betrayed by a vacant stare or wandering eyes.

We all want to know that what we say and think matters. But if we want others to care about what we say, we need to show we care about what they say. Like all the important virtues, we teach respect best by demonstrating it. So listen up! It will make people feel better and you may even learn something.

Respect Means Knowing When to Back Off

I've addressed the ethical obligation to treat others with respect by attentive listening. Now I want to talk about the flip side of respect, the duty to back off and accept the fact that listening doesn't require agreeing.

The problem is especially prevalent in relationships where a person in authority, say a boss or parent, lectures, criticizes, sermonizes or even berates an employee or child well past the point of legitimate communication. But bulldozer conversations can also be launched by anyone who seeks to impose an idea on someone else.

The common thread in disrespectful communications is that they go beyond reasonable attempts to inform or even persuade — they become harangues. It's as if the speaker is engaged in a campaign to beat us into submission rather than simply convey a point of view. So he or she pummels us with repetitive opinions, complaints or demands. And if we don't give the desired response, the speaker simply restates the point more loudly or aggressively.

Telling one of these ardent opinionators that we understand their position, that we've really heard and considered what they have had to say, rarely stops the onslaught, because the only way some people will believe that we understand their point is if we agree with it. They can become so self-righteous that they truly believe that disagreement with them is proof of confusion, ignorance, stupidity or closed-mindedness.

No one has a right to impose his opinions on others or to demand that he be listened to until he is done. The moral obligation of respect requires that we learn when to back off just as we learn when to listen.

A General Talks of Moral Courage

Several years ago, Gen. Charles C. Krulak, then commandant of the Marine Corps, addressed a college graduating class. He spoke of character and courage. His insights were profound.

"Success . . . has always demanded . . . character," he declared, adding, "Those who can reach . . . within themselves and draw upon an inner strength, fortified by strong values, always carry the day against those of lesser character. Moral cowards never win."

He went on to urge graduates to face up to the ethical challenges of their daily lives and "make moral courage a habit so that [you] will be ready for the greater tests of character."

His conclusion was especially eloquent: "When the test of your character and moral courage comes — regardless of the noise and confusion around you — there will be a moment of inner silence in which you must decide what to do. Your character will be defined by your decision . . . and it is yours and yours alone to make. When that moment comes, think of this poem by an unknown author. It is called the "The Eagle and the Wolf":

There is a great battle that rages inside me.
One side is a soaring eagle.
Everything the eagle stands for is good and true and beautiful.
It soars above the clouds.
Even though it dips down into the valleys, it lays its eggs on the mountain tops.
The other side of me is a howling wolf.
And that raging, howling wolf represents the worst that is in me.
He eats upon my downfalls and justifies himself by his presence in the pack.
Who wins this great battle?
The one I feed.

Michael Josephson

The Value of
Self-Sufficiency

What ever happened to self-sufficiency, self-reliance and independence as treasured goals of youth? It used to seem so natural. As young children learn how to feed and dress themselves, most parents are confronted with the adamant demand: "I want to do it myself." It's a huge source of pride to experience the first waves of independence.

Yet somewhere along the line, the budding idea that self-sufficiency is a desirable, even pleasurable state is replaced by an entitlement-dependence mentality. And what we get is too many young people who are comfortable with their hands out and indifferent to the idea of keeping their heads high.

It's troubling how few young people seem to understand the power, even the glory, of self-sufficiency. We need to do a better job of teaching that self-sufficiency is a good thing, even if it means doing with less.

Self-sufficiency is the only road to true independence and personal freedom. Dependency always comes with strings attached. We also need to emphasize that self-sufficiency is a matter of character and an important aspect of responsibility.

People of character try to carry their own weight. They want to free others of the burden of providing for them. It's not a moral flaw to fall short of this goal, but it is if it's not taken seriously and pursued with authentic best efforts.

Self-sufficiency is not simply a state of financial independence wished for by parents anxious to reclaim their incomes and homes. Self-sufficiency is, or at least should be, a genuinely prized source of self-respect and esteem, arising from the sense of freedom that comes with knowing that we can thrive on our own, without relying on the good will and resources of others.

Living a Good Life in the Pursuit of Happiness

See to do good, and you will find that happiness will run after you.

James Freeman Clarke

Live Backwards

Ben just came to town as a new pastor. Unfortunately, his first official duty was to conduct a funeral service for Albert, a man who died in his eighties with no relatives. Since Ben didn't know the deceased personally, he paused from his sermon to ask if anyone in the congregation would say something good about Albert. There was no response. Ben asked again: "Many of you knew Albert for years. Surely someone can say something nice." After an uncomfortable pause, a voice from the back of the room said, "Well, his brother was worse."

If you died tomorrow, what would people say about you? Would it make you proud of the way you lived and the choices you made?

Thinking about the legacy we leave can help us keep our priorities straight. Few people would be satisfied with an epitaph like: "She always got what she wanted." Or: "He never missed a deadline."

There's an old saying, "If you want to know how to live your life, think about what you'd like people to say about you after you die . . . and live backwards." The idea is that we earn our eulogy by our everyday choices.

In his book *When Everything You Ever Wanted Isn't Enough* Harold Kushner writes, "Our souls are not hungry for fame, comfort, wealth or power. Our souls are hungry for meaning, for the sense that we have figured out how to live so that our lives matter, so that the world will be at least a little bit different for our having passed through it."

The Be-a-Better-Person Diet

Often I'm told I'm just preaching to the choir. After all, anyone willing to listen to all my chatter about character is probably more ethical than the average person. Am I wasting my time? I don't think so. First, I believe that you don't have to be sick to get better. No matter how relatively good we are, our character can be strengthened. Second, it's just as important to spur a good person to be better as it is to induce a bad person to change his ways.

So wherever you are on the character spectrum, consider starting a "Be a Better Person" fitness program. It involves exercise and dieting. The exercise part asks you to do more good things and the dieting part challenges you to do less of the not-so-good things. It's based on the Six Pillars of Character. Work on toning your moral muscles one pillar each day. On the seventh day you can rest.

Monday, start with trustworthiness. Look out for little lies and deceptions. Be especially careful to keep your commitments. Tuesday, work on responsibility. Be scrupulously accountable. Go the extra mile to pursue excellence. Wednesday, concentrate on treating people with respect. Avoid put-downs, gossip and impatience. Be a better listener. Be especially courteous. Thursday, pay attention to fairness. Don't jump to conclusions. Be sure you're open-minded. Friday, focus on caring. Be extra kind and generous. Share. Saturday is about being a good citizen. Don't break rules, even little ones. Do something for your community. Recycle. Then, start again on Monday.

These little acts will not only make you a better person. They'll make a better world.

Michael Josephson

Setting up a "Me" File

During a dinner with close friends, I shared an e-mail I'd just received from a 13-year-old who wanted to thank me for the way my commentaries had influenced his life. He said lots of nice things, and I was clearly proud of the note. Sally, one of our dinner companions, suggested that I put it in a "Me" file.

I asked her what she meant. She told me of a practice she developed working with in-home nurses who, she said, often live isolated and lonely lives. During orientation training, Sally would give each nurse an empty folder labeled "Me." She instructed the nurses to put into the file every form of positive feedback including notes, letters and positive performance reviews. This "Me" folder should be looked at whenever they questioned the value of their work or felt unappreciated.

Sally said that while almost all the nurses eventually came to use and really like the idea of the "Me" file, they were initially reluctant. They feared it would appear too self-indulgent and egotistical. After all, nursing was supposed to be selfless.

Well, I think the "Me" file is a terrific idea. Everyone should have one. It's not a bragging file to show others how good we are, but a private collection of the small triumphs that give us psychic gratification and reconnect us with the best reasons we do what we do.

The next step is to conduct ourselves in such a way that keeps the "Me" file full.

The Gas Can Scam

Jim and Sheryl were newly married and on a limited budget, living in Chicago. A tall red-headed man approached them with an empty gas can. "I'm stranded. Could you spare $5 so I could get gas?" he asked. "If you'll give me your address I'll send it back to you."

"Of course," Sheryl said. "You may need a few more dollars. Here's a ten. Good luck!"

Jim rolled his eyes but Sheryl shrugged, "He needed help."

A week later, Jim was reading the paper over breakfast when he burst out laughing. Apparently a tall red-headed man had been arrested for approaching people with an empty gas can and asking for $5. It was a scam. The police found 28 five dollar bills in his pocket — and one ten dollar bill. Jim laughed. "The ten might as well have had your name on it," he told Sheryl. "That's what you get for giving money to everyone with a sob story."

Was Sheryl a fool? I don't think so. Sure, she was victimized by a clever crook. But what's the alternative? Should we let conscienceless creeps harden our hearts to pleas for help?

The downside risk of being suckered occasionally is vastly outweighed by the risk that, in our cynicism, we will turn our backs on someone who is truly in need. I'd rather be wrong than heartless.

The day we stop helping one another in order to guarantee not being taken advantage of is the day that evil wins. Of course our kindness will keep cons and cheats in business, but we can live with that. When our motives are pure, we should be able to live with the embarrassment of being played for a fool. What we can't accept is a society where caring and compassion shrivel under our suspicions.

Finding God in the Park

Aaron was 80 and he was losing his memory. Against his will he moved in with his son, who cared about him but tended to treat him as a child. The old man missed his independence, including spending time in a park that was near his old apartment but more than a mile away from his son's home. One Saturday he decided to find his old park. Without his son's knowledge, he took some cheese and a couple of bananas and set off.

Soon, he became lost. When he saw a boy about eight, he asked the young fellow where the park was. The boy, who said his name was Timmy, said, "I'd take you there, but I'm looking for God. I've got to talk to him about why my parents are getting a divorce."

The old man said, "Maybe God is in the park. I'd like to talk to him too about why he's made me useless." And so they set off together. Aaron took Timmy to his favorite bench and shared his bananas and cheese. When Timmy began to cry about the divorce, Aaron lovingly held his face in both hands and looked him right in the eyes. "Timmy, I don't know why bad things happen, but I know it's not your fault and that you are going to be OK."

"Are you sure?" the boy asked.

"Yes, I'm sure. Whatever comes, you can deal with it."

On the walk back, Timmy said, "I don't know why you think you are useless. I think you are wonderful." They parted with a warm hug.

Timmy's mom saw the man and boy part, and she asked her son, "Who was that old man?"

"He's God," Timmy said.

"Did he say that?" she said skeptically.

"No, but I know it was God because when he hugged me, he made everything OK."

Many blocks away Aaron's son caught up with his father and demanded, "Dad, where have you been? I've been looking all over for you!"

"I was talking with God," Aaron said.

"What makes you think you talked to God?" his son replied scornfully.

"Because when he touched me I realized that I may not be everything I used to be, but I'm not useless."

Michael Josephson

Happiness
Is a Choice

In a "Peanuts" cartoon, Lucy asks Charlie Brown, "Why do you think we were put on earth?" Charlie answers, "To make others happy."

"I don't think I'm making anyone happy," Lucy replies, "but nobody's making me very happy either. Somebody's not doing his job!"

Charlie talked about life in terms of giving, while Lucy only thought about getting. I know a lot of people like Lucy. Preoccupied with getting and having, they are so aware of what they don't have that they never enjoy what they do. They live in an "if only" world, always at least one step away from happiness. "If only I could get this raise, make this sale, pay off my debts, win this game, I'd be happy."

Dennis Prager, in his book *Happiness Is a Serious Problem*, argues that human nature itself impedes our ability to be happy. He claims that children learn to demand "more" as soon as they begin to communicate, and that the desire for more can never be satisfied because the more we have, the more we want.

Abraham Lincoln, who was prone toward depression, said, "A person is generally about as happy as he's willing to be." He understood that happiness is a way of looking at your life. It's about choosing good feelings over bad, positive attitudes over negative ones and gratitude over greed. Thus, people who are poor, ugly and in ill health can be considerably happier than people who are rich, beautiful and healthy — because they choose to be.

Happiness is not getting what we want; it's learning to want what we get.

Winning the Lottery Won't Bring Happiness

Many philosophers believe that happiness is the sole criterion for a successful life. So it's not surprising that a huge amount of human energy is spent in the pursuit of happiness. And, despite lofty aphorisms to the contrary, many people believe that money buys happiness and, therefore, that cash is more important than character.

The facts belie this shallow philosophy. For example, research shows that while lottery winners gain a temporary jolt of joy from their winnings, generally they are not happier in the long run. The euphoria of new activities and possessions is almost as short-lived as a drug-induced high and, what's worse, the suddenly-rich often experience less pleasure from activities they previously enjoyed.

According to Dr. David G. Myers, it's not just lottery winners who discover the false promise of wealth. One study of Americans worth at least $100 million showed that even the extremely rich are only slightly more happy than average. Yesterday's luxuries become today's necessities and tomorrow's relics.

But the real shocker is that victims of disabling tragedies resulting in blindness or paralysis, people who must cope every day of their lives with potentially devastating limitations, generally recover emotionally, and in just a few years, their level of happiness is just about the same as their able-bodied contemporaries.

Apparently, humans have an enormous capacity to adapt to fame, fortune and affliction. Adaptation becomes a mechanism that drains the pleasure out of great good fortune and the despair out of horrible misfortune. So if major life events, whether good or bad, have minimal influence on long-term life satisfaction, what's a person to do? The answer is simple: stop chasing shadows and realize that the real road to happiness is paved with quality relationships and the sense of worthiness that comes from good character.

Character in the Workplace

*Goodness is the
only investment
that never fails.*

Henry David Thoreau

There's No Such Thing as Business Ethics

During a workshop for a Fortune 100 company, I made what I thought was an uncontroversial point that beyond a legal obligation to keep promises and honor contracts, there is an ethical duty; it's a part of being trustworthy. A senior executive objected strenuously.

"Whether the company wants to live up to its commitments is a business decision, not an ethical one," he said. In fact, he said, the company had a responsibility to evaluate whether it was in its best interests to honor or breach contracts, and the decision should be based on a simple cost/benefit analysis. Ethics was not an issue.

Under this theory, whatever works is right. It makes the pursuit of self-interest the proper standard for business judgments. This theory of "business ethics" flourishes because many people compartmentalize their lives into personal and business domains, assuming each is governed by different standards of ethics. In business, the argument goes, ethical principles like trustworthiness, respect, responsibility, fairness, caring and good citizenship are simply factors to be taken into account. They're not moral obligations.

As a result, fundamentally good people, who would never lie, cheat or break a promise in their personal lives, delude themselves into thinking that they can properly do so in business. This rationale is fatally flawed.

Ethics is not concerned with descriptions of the way things are but prescriptions for the way they ought to be. Though we may face different sorts of ethical challenges at work, the standards do not change when we enter the workplace. There is no such thing as "business ethics" — there is only ethics.

Integrity Is a Personal Asset

I saw a cartoon of an earnest-looking fellow standing in front of a man sitting behind a desk. The caption: "We admire your integrity, Daniel. Unfortunately, we have no room for that in our firm." This may not be an overstatement.

A 1995 survey of more than 2,000 secretaries in the U.S. and Canada revealed that nearly 60 percent had lied about their supervisors' whereabouts. OK, that's a moral misdemeanor, but nearly one in five also said they had falsely stated they witnessed a signature on a notarized document, and 10 percent said they had removed or destroyed damaging information from a file at the request of their bosses.

Usually, the lies and deceptions told at work aren't company policy. Instead, they reflect the flexible morality of individual supervisors who, out of ambition, fear or corrupt character, ask others to lie or look the other way.

Let there be no mistake: it's unethical to ask someone to lie to advance personal or business objectives. Executives should establish an environment where every employee is expected to be honest. And they must deal firmly and consistently with those who ask or allow employees to do otherwise. But it's also the responsibility of individual employees, regardless of their power or status, to exercise the moral courage to refuse to do anything unethical, even when ordered to do so. Your integrity is a personal asset. Don't let anyone mess with it.

The Crossroads

There comes a time in most people's lives when they become aware of how hard it can be to meet all the demands and needs of work and family. It isn't easy to find a balance. A metaphor I wrote as part of a graduation address for lawyers may provide a helpful perspective.

"As you leave school to truly enter the world, imagine that you are at a crossroads of two mountain paths," I wrote. "One is marked Career, the other Life. The road called Career is steep and a bit treacherous, but it leads directly to the pinnacle called Success. There you'll find all the things you can get with money, power and prestige.

"The road called Life has more ups, downs and turns and it continually branches into new crossroads. Some roads lead to dead ends and others to mountain streams and glorious vistas. The funny thing about this road is that there is no top, no final destination. Life is the road itself.

"At first, the Career road looks more tempting. The rewards are attractive — especially to those tired of feeling poor and burdened with debt — but in many ways it's less demanding. All one has to do is concentrate on work. And because complicated and time-consuming things like love, service to others and spiritual growth are generally considered distractions, those who reach the mountaintop often do so alone or with damaged or shallow relationships.

"Family, friends, fun and faith are much more important on the road called Life. In fact, they're indispensable. The most proficient travelers on this road have careers, but they find ways to make their work meaningful and enjoyable. They believe a career can help them have a good life, but they never allow their lives to be defined only by their careers. They find ways to integrate love and laughter into the way they make a living.

"One advantage of the Life road is that you can pause at any plateau or viewing-point and experience fulfillment, a very different kind of feeling than success. And the really great thing is that you don't have to wait to reach the top. You can feel fulfilled anytime you pause to reflect on where you are and where you've been.

"My advice: choose Life!"

Honor Will Find a Way

As I reflect on the interview process that's such a vital part of the mating ritual between employers and job applicants, I'm struck by how important and rare complete honesty is. These interviews are like early courtship conversations where both parties are so anxious to please and impress that they exaggerate everything that might be desirable and disguise whatever might displease.

Let's face it. It's hard to be honest when the truth may be an obstacle to something we want. And honesty is not only about telling the literal truth, but about conveying the truth. So calculated deceptions and nondisclosures of important facts are just as bad as lies.

Thus, company representatives who fail to disclose serious financial problems, or the intent to close a division in the near future, are just as dishonest as applicants who fail to mention that they intend to go to grad school or move out of state within a year, or that they view the job as a stopgap economic necessity and will continually be looking for something better.

Yes, indeed, telling the whole truth is often a disadvantage. That's why it takes character to live with integrity. I know it's customary in business to manipulate people and situations to gain an advantage, but it isn't right. We can try to disarm our consciences by thinking of the world in terms of dog-eat-dog or simply as a rat race, but in the end, remember what Lily Tomlin said: "The problem with the rat race is that even if you win, you're still a rat."

It's not the easy road but people of integrity can survive because honor will always find a way.

The First Question: Is It Ethical?

When faced with a difficult decision, business executives are commonly taught to first ask themselves whether the conduct in question is legal. If it isn't, they're instructed to abandon the option and comply with the law. If the conduct is legal, then they're told to consider whether it's ethical.

In the wake of the massive unethical conduct by Enron executives, accountants and lawyers, we kept hearing about the complexity of the issues. We were led to believe that the laws and regulations in this area are so complex that the Enron bosses were shrouded in endless shades of gray. Give me a break!

The first question to ask is not whether the conduct is legal but whether it's ethical. This forces decision makers to think about actions in terms of moral principles like honesty, responsibility and fairness without regard to rationalizations and interpretations trying to justify the conduct as legal.

We don't need a lawyer's opinion or an accounting regulation to know that partnerships conceived for the sole purpose of deceiving people about the true financial position of a company are fundamentally dishonest and unethical. We don't need professionals to tell us it's irresponsible to build up an incredibly large debt that jeopardizes the pension funds of tens of thousands of employees and the financial stability of creditors and vendors, or that paying huge salaries and bonuses to the executives who drove the country's seventh largest company into bankruptcy, while freezing the right of employees to sell Enron stock from their 401(k) plans, is unfair and unethical. And if it's unethical, it's wrong! The legalities are entirely irrelevant.

Remember, there's a big difference between what one has a right to do and what is right to do. Hiding behind legal schemes and excuses may keep these guys out of jail but it will also keep them out of heaven.

Just Ask Your Grandmother

Huge companies like Enron and Global Crossing have recently been brought down by massive dishonesty, irresponsible debt and shameless self-dealing. The more we learn about these situations, the more likely we are to conclude that moral compromise is an integral part of corporate life.

It seems that lying is simply a necessary tactic for executives driven on the one hand by a lust for vast rewards, and on the other by an abiding fear of losing their place at the table. And, lower down in the corporation, it seems many workers just want to keep their jobs, so they do what they're told.

It's doubtlessly true that in some companies it is really hard to consistently do the right thing. But temptation is not moral ambiguity. Today's executive can go through hundreds of pages of laws and spend hundreds of thousands of dollars on lawyers and accountants to find ways to justify conduct that every grandmother knows is flat-out wrong.

The greatest defense against scandal and disgrace is not an army of lawyers and accountants, but simple integrity. Just be honest! Don't make this more difficult than it is. White lies may be acceptable, trading off honesty for kindness in certain social situations (e.g., telling your wife she doesn't look a day older, or your husband that you love the ugly sweater he bought), but don't use these examples to justify self-serving business lies to inflate profits, conceal problems or evade laws.

I challenge you to think of a situation where it's ethical to lie for a business purpose. And, by the way, clever deceivers are no better than liars. Ask your grandmother.

There's more to life than profits and promotions. For the sake of your family and your peace of mind, don't let the cynics convince you that honest people can't survive in business. In fact, the way things are going, integrity is likely to be the most treasured quality in the next decade.

Michael Josephson

In Business and Sports the Solution Is Character

Tell someone you're going to write a book on business ethics and they're likely to sneer something like, "It's going to be a short book." Say it's about sports ethics and you'll get a similar response. Though I hate this sort of cynicism, we've got to admit that when the going gets tough, an awful lot of people adopt a dog-eat-dog mentality that views ethics as an unrealistic handicap.

In business, goals are stated in terms of profits or productivity; in sports it's medals or victories. With the message "If you don't get results we'll get someone else who can" ringing in their ears, too many managers and coaches give in to a sort of survival paranoia that yields to look-out-for-number-one and win-at-any-cost strategies that spawn all sorts of moral compromise. And each compromiser says he or she had no choice: It's the system.

What happened to the idea of moral courage? Why are so many talented men and women so desperate to keep their jobs that they don't care what the jobs make of them? It's troublesome enough when we see topflight managers collapse under competitive pressures, but it's especially disheartening when we see the supposed guardians of the noble traditions of sport surrender to fear, ambition and greed.

The inspirational spirit of athletic competition captured in the Olympic ideal is too often lost in a grubby survival-of-the-fittest free-for-all, where the operative philosophy is "do whatever you can get away with."

It's no use to describe the problem as irresistible "pressures" created by escalating goals and intense competition. Pressures are just temptations in disguise, and all temptations are resistible. The problem is one of character. When the only way to win — which is just another way of saying "getting what we want" — is to lie, cheat or otherwise dishonor oneself, a person of character would rather lose. You see, there's much more at stake than a job.

Character and Sports

The most important decision I ever made in my career was to live my life in sports as honestly and ethically as possible.
Greg LeMond

We Should Expect More From Adults

Rick's 11-year-old son Mark was in a youth baseball league. He was not highly skilled and was easily discouraged, but Rick urged him to stay with the program. "Just do your best," he said. "That's all anyone can ask and your best is good enough." So the boy persisted.

The league had a rule that everyone plays. Mark played but regularly struck out at the plate and made errors in the field. When Mark struck out his first time at bat, Rick struggled to look positive. Later, Mark hit a hard grounder to third. It was close, but Rick was sure Mark beat the throw. When the umpire, a volunteer parent, called Mark out, Rick went wild. "Hey, Zebra!" he yelled. "Are you blind, stupid or is the other team paying you?"

The umpire looked over at Rick, who couldn't seem to control his growing rage.

"You're an idiot," Rick added. "If you can't do the job, stay off the field!"

On the way home, Mark was unusually quiet. Finally, he said, "Dad, I thought you said, 'Doing your best is good enough.'"

"It is," Rick assured him. "You were safe that last time. You were robbed by a bad call."

"I wasn't talking about me," Mark replied. "I was talking about the umpire, Billy's dad. I know he was doing his best but you got really mad at him."

"Yeah, son, but he's an adult and we should expect more out of adults."

Mark looked his dad right in the eye and said, "That's what I thought too. By the way, I was out."

Rick's good intentions just weren't enough. We expect more from adults — more fairness and respect, more sportsmanship and more self-restraint. If your kids play sports, be a model, not a problem.

Michael Josephson

The Ennobling Qualities of the Olympics

I attended the 1996 Olympic Games in Atlanta and saw some incredible performances. I also witnessed instances of bad sportsmanship, disqualifications for drug use, and excesses in commercialization and materialism that mocked Olympic ideals.

The Olympic Creed holds that the most important thing is not to win but to take part, not to conquer, but to fight well. In blasphemous rejection of this credo, Nike posters around the venue proclaimed, "You don't win the silver, you lose the gold."

But despite grounds for cynicism, I refuse to let the horde of barbarians who are looting the temples that house Olympic ideals destroy my ability to appreciate the momentous drama of the finest athletes on the planet struggling to perform at their very best — to be faster, stronger and more graceful than anyone has ever been. And when a new world record is set, I will marvel not only because I've seen history made, but because I've witnessed human potential redefined.

Remember, despite the widespread materialism and constant hype, thousands of Olympians were filled with pride when a torch-bearing fellow athlete opened the Games reciting an oath for all to honor: "In the name of all competitors, I promise to take part in these Olympic Games . . . in the true spirit of sportsmanship, for the glory of sport and the honor of our teams."

Just as these athletes are ennobled by their pursuit of victory with honor, so can we uplift our lives by pursuing our own goals with dedication, optimism and honor.

Michael Josephson

144

Youth Sports and the Olympic Games

I n February 2002, with the Winter Olympics as the backdrop, the Josephson Institute
hosted a summit meeting of many of the
most influential leaders in youth sports. Their
task was to develop standards and strategies to
improve the quality of the sports experience for
youngsters 12 and under. Before coming up with
a document called "Gold Medal Standards for
Youth Sports," a lot of time was spent discussing
bad sportsmanship, violent and abusive parent behavior, and other negative trends that demean and
diminish the reputation and reality of youth sports.

At the same time, the growing gap between
Olympic ideals and some ugly realities of modern
day competition did not go unnoticed. In both
youth and Olympic sports, the divide between
noble rhetoric and nasty reality results from an

abandonment of the gallant and uplifting goals of athletic competition in favor of an unrestrained, obsessive and often unprincipled pursuit of personal glory and material gain.

Though the word "competition" is derived from the Latin word *competere*, which embodies the idea of "striving together," competitors are commonly viewed as enemies, even in a youth context. Instead of striving for personal excellence and pursuing victory with honor, modern soldiers of sport want to win so badly that they shamelessly engage in aggressive, hostile, disrespectful and dishonest behavior.

The solution is easy to articulate, but hard to achieve. We have to take to heart the Olympic Creed: "The most important thing is not to win but to take part, just as the most important thing in life is not the triumph, but the struggle. The essential thing is not to have conquered, but to have fought well."

You see, real sports is not about defeating someone else. It's about having fun and improving yourself. If there are enemies in sports, they are the people who are pillaging its noble traditions.

The Essence of Sportsmanship

In 1964, an Italian named Eugenio Monti was the world champion in bobsledding and a strong favorite in the Winter Olympics. His nation expected a gold medal and after his last run it looked as if he might get it. The British team, led by Tony Nash, still had a chance to beat him, but Nash discovered a faulty axle that would require his team to withdraw. Instead, Monti removed a critical bolt from his sled and offered it to Nash.

As if to prove that no good deed goes unpunished, Nash won the gold medal and Monti was viciously criticized in the Italian press. Yet he was unshaken. "Nash didn't win because I gave him the bolt," he reportedly said. "He won because he had the fastest run."

Every real competitor wants to win, but Olympic medallist John Naber says a true sportsman, one who believes in the Olympic ideal, wants to win against his best opponent on his best day. The sportsman is not elated but disappointed when top competitors are injured or disqualified.

Monti won the gold medal at the next Winter Olympics, but it was his willingness to lose that earned him a prominent place in Olympic history. His act represents sportsmanship at its best: the pursuit of victory with zeal and passion, recognizing that there is no true victory without honor.

Today, with so many athletes willing to cheat or behave badly just to win, we need reminders of the noble potential of sports. And parents and coaches should be teaching youngsters that the real glory of sport is in the striving, not the winning.

Earning My Letter

When I entered Westchester High School as a tenth-grader, I wanted to play basketball in the worst way. Unfortunately, that was the only way I could play. I was very small and I couldn't dribble, jump or shoot very well. But I was enthusiastic and never missed a practice. I hustled and I made the C team as a third-stringer. Undaunted, I was determined to earn a letterman's jacket.

To do this, I had to play in a total of 12 quarters during the season. Since it didn't matter how long you played, I always sat by Coach Saunders, and when there were six or eight seconds left in a quarter, I asked to go in. I think my total playing time for the year was about a minute and fifty seconds, but every time I got in the game I was determined to make something happen. Invariably, I lunged for the ball and usually committed a foul. I'm sure I must have had the highest foul-per-second ratio ever recorded. Still, by the end of the season I had played in exactly 12 quarters. I earned my letter and was ecstatic.

I grew a bit in the next few years, and by my senior year I was a starter — still for the C team. That was enough for me. I got good grades and several academic honors, but I was proudest of earning my letter for three years running.

Thinking back on those years, I realize how lucky I was to have a coach who gave me a chance to feel like a winner. If you coach or teach youngsters, I hope you'll find a way to give each child the kind of memories my coach gave me.

Michael Josephson

The Hijacking of High School Sports

As an athlete, I had to aspire to be mediocre. Still I loved sports, and when, at age 13, my baseball career ended because I was cut from my Pony League team, it was a devastating blow. Fortunately, my high school had a different philosophy: every kid who wanted to participate could have a sports experience. So they had four levels from varsity to C team. I switched to basketball, and though I rode the bench my first year for all but about two minutes, I had a great experience. I stayed on the C team as a senior and became a starter.

I believe that sports belong in schools as an important opportunity for physical and social growth. But high school sports are being hijacked. A minority of competitive coaches and a growing contingent of sports parents, consumed by their illusions of professional careers for their kids, have changed the face of interscholastic competition. As the pursuit of celebrity, glory and imagined financial rewards has pushed the educational values of competing far out of sight, schools all over the country are violating the spirit of sportsmanship and abandoning the value of balanced competition by assembling all-star teams of elite athletes.

But it's not the athletes that are exploited. These kids and their parents are getting exactly what they want. The real victims are the teams they wallop because of the mismatch, and the kids who want to play but are displaced by students who transfer from other schools, often other countries. Today, few highly successful programs are built on local kids.

It's a shame and a sham and I don't understand why the parents of the kids who are denied their chance to play for their school tolerate it.

Heroes, Models and Just Good People

What is important is not what happens to us, but how we respond to what happens to us.

Jean-Paul Sartre

Lauren the Cheerful

I have a confession to make: I used to think that really cheerful people were either simple-minded or led simple lives with no problems. It would really bug me when I was clearly being pressed by problems, and some self-appointed cheer bug would say perkily, "Cheer up." What did they think? I liked being worried or grumpy? Didn't they understand that I couldn't help it? I was genetically disposed to worry and, besides, I really had a lot to be worried about!

But for the last few years I've been working under the influence of Lauren, my administrative assistant and chief of staff (actually she refers to herself as the "chief of stuff"). She's a cheermeister of the highest order. But she defies my stereotype. She's certainly not simple-minded, and she has health problems from recurring cancer that could topple a substantial tree.

The difference between Lauren and most other people I know is that she has developed the herculean strength and courage that beat negative thoughts into retreat. In a sense, her cheerfulness is an act of willful defiance and strategy to squeeze the best out of herself and her precious life.

And the thing that really gets me is that her positive attitude, just the upbeat tone of her voice, really works. She makes me feel better and stronger. I'm not nearly in her league, but I do appreciate the contagious power of good cheer. Now I realize it's not an act of naïveté but an act of kindness to be cheerful. It's a gift to others.

I know I can't always control how I feel inside, but I can choose the face I show to the world. When I choose to be positive I begin to feel positive. And so do others around me. I don't know how Lauren does it, but my strategy is simple: all I have to do is randomly think of any one of my children — and my heart smiles.

Michael Josephson

Jason's Tribute and Making a Difference

Just a few days after the terrorist attacks of September 11, 2001, I was referred to a web site on the Internet (www.cantcryhardenough.com) by someone who thought I would be moved by the beautiful photographic and musical tribute to the heroes and victims of that tragic day. She was right. The moving montage of photos was backed by a song called "I Can't Cry Hard Enough" written by David Williams & Marvin Etzioni, and performed by Victoria Williams. The opening lines captured and created the mood of mourning:

> *I'm going to live my life*
> *Like every day's my last*
> *Without a simple good-bye*
> *It all goes by so fast*
> *And now that you're gone*
> *I can't cry hard enough*

I was so impressed, I wanted to know who was behind this, so I wrote to the address on the website and asked for a phone number so I could talk to the creator. And so I met Jason Powers, a 24-year-old artist and musician in Corona, California, who said he was so overwhelmed by emotion that he had to do something.

He worked almost without stop gathering photos and designing the website. He even got permission of the artists to use the music. When he finished he e-mailed a link of his tribute to 25 people. That's all, 25 people. Within a week his web page became so overloaded it was shut down. A few days later he opened a new one that could handle the traffic of more than 100,000 visitors per day. Within a month, more than 2 million people had experienced Jason's tribute.

I was inspired not only by Jason's heart and talent, but by the astonishingly powerful confirmation of the cliché that one person can make a difference. This one young man touched the lives of millions of strangers, and he's not done yet.

Cynics worry so much about what can't be done that they never understand what can be

— *continued on next page* —

Michael Josephson

done. Edward Everett Hale said, "It's true I am only one, but I am one. And the fact that I cannot do everything must not prevent me from doing what I can do." Jason's story reminds us not to underestimate how much that is.

I hope I shall always possess firmness and virtue enough to maintain what I consider the most enviable of all titles, the character of an "honest man."

George Washington

A Doctor
Who Cares

Dr. Fred Epstein specializes in children with brain tumors. He's one of the best in the world but, as good as he is, he regularly has to deal with youngsters he can't save. And when these patients die he must deal with parents whose grief and pain can shatter souls. So it wouldn't be surprising if the good doctor retreated behind a wall of professional objectivity to shield himself from the emotions of death and dying.

But he doesn't. Instead, he makes a special effort to be sure that he and his associates never lose sight of the humanity of his patients. According to an article in *Modern Maturity*, while Dr. Epstein was addressing a conference, he unfolded a piece of paper. It was a poem from a teenage boy found by his parents after he died:

Why do I live?
I have prayed in the night
By the cold and lonely side of my bed...
And I still wonder: Will I be saved?
I ask you, reader, whoever you may be,
Take my trembling hand and warm it with
Care and sympathy.

"I always felt I failed this boy," he said. "I kept thinking of his line about sitting alone in a cold room and there's no one to hold his hand. And I thought: We doctors have been arrogant. We've been so focused on technology that we haven't paid attention to what the living person is going through."

So, when he had the chance to start an institute for neurology at a prominent New York hospital, he dedicated himself to creating an environment pervaded with genuine caring and love.

"Please don't let me die," a boy pleaded before a surgery. When he began the operation he announced to his colleagues, "This is a 10-year-old boy from a small Southern town. His parents love him a lot. He's an only child, and he plays soccer. Let's make sure he'll play soccer again."

Michael Josephson

Tuesdays With Morrie

Real wisdom is often hard to appreciate. The problem is that so many of the most potent and elegant insights from philosophy, literature and scripture have been presented and processed in commencement addresses, political speeches, calendars, wall hangings and greeting cards that we tend to think of them as commercialized clichés. We may recognize them, but few of us take the time to understand these profound observations.

Occasionally, someone repackages some of these truths in a way that reaches us on a such a deep level that it reshapes our values and influences our actions. I think this is the case with *Tuesdays With Morrie*, a marvelous book by Mitch Albom and a poignant television movie that reaches the mind through the heart. It's the true story of Morrie Schwartz, an extraordinary teacher who, knowing he was dying of Lou Gehrig's disease, shared candid reflections on living and dying in weekly sessions with a former student.

Among other things, Morrie tells us that aging is not just decay, but growth, and that knowing you are going to die isn't all bad. "Understanding that you will die," he says, "helps you live a better life." He asks four key questions: "Have you found someone to share your heart with? Are you giving to your community? Are you at peace with yourself? Are you trying to be as human as you can be?" He talks about the Buddhist concept of living each day with the realization that it could be our last, and urges us to overcome self-defeating selfishness and hidden fears that cause us to waste our lives on meaningless activities and petty resentments. "Forgive everyone everything right now," he suggests. And don't be afraid to love. "Dying ends life," he says, "not relationships," and he teaches us by word and example the profound and lasting joy of love and friendship.

John Wooden's 91st Birthday

One of my personal heroes turned 91 recently. He's not a general or a politician or a movie star. He's a teacher. Oh, I'll admit he's not an ordinary teacher. He's also the world's most successful and famous basketball coach. But John Wooden is, above all, a teacher. He's also a classic homespun philosopher.

His thoughts and theories have been recorded in dozens of books, but reading John Wooden doesn't hold a candle to hearing from the man himself. His words are amplified by his extraordinary character.

You don't just meet the Coach; you experience him. The man exudes an inner dignity and moral strength that makes you feel both worthy and humble at the same time.

Integrity, respect and kindness pervade everything he says. But more striking, it seems so effortless. He has received more awards and accolades than any 10 of his peers, yet he is genuinely humble. I had to insist that he call me by my first name so he'd stop calling me Mr. Josephson. He talks about issues of honor, hard work, preparation and self-discipline as if there were no other choices.

This both inspires and humbles me. You see, for me, trying to be a person of character involves a daily struggle. Sometimes it feels as if I am acting the part of a good person rather than really being one. I don't think I will ever be as gracefully authentic as Coach Wooden. Yet if I told him this, I think he would smile and say something like, "Michael, never underestimate what you can do. Why don't you keep trying? You'll get better."

Michael Josephson

To subscribe to a free e-mail newsletter of Mr. Josephson's commentaries, please send an e-mail (with "subscribe" in the subject line) to commentary@jiethics.org.

For an archive of recent commentaries, as well as information about the Josephson Institute and its various projects, please visit www.charactercounts.org.